SYSTEM INVERSION

KAREN KELLOCK PH.D.

**Manual for
Superior Men**

**A complete theory based on Einstein physics,
Political Psychology, Systems Theory
and Archetypal Psychiatry.**

**FORMULA
All success attraction
All disease obstruction
All recovery elimination**

**You must fast on all three
OBSTRUCTIONS:
People
Habit
Food**

SYSTEM INVERSION

It was like putting a rattlesnake in your cage but in naïve victim denial you couldn't see it, ok? If too weak to keep boundaries the evil world flows in and like a Tsunami it'll ruin you surely. It's the Fallen Hero Syndrome when previous fans become foes as you're goin' down. As long as they're around you're adapting to THEM. Empaths easily become doormats for other's ends. You're such a strong beach they see the light and cling on. It's sad so stay detached son.

SYSTEM INVERSION

BULIMIA AND OTHER SYMPTOMS
BOUNDARIES ARE ALL
"NO" THE MOST IMPORTANT WORD
TRAUMA BRINGS MORAL COLLAPSE
WIFE OF ALCOHOLIC SYNDROME
LESSONS CAN BE SHOCKING
POWERLESS POWER PLAYS
QUEEN MAKES IT PASSED THE BLOCKS
LIVING WITH A RATTLESNAKE
THE HIGH CLASS WINO
MORE TROUBLE THAN THEY'RE WORTH
THEY'RE MEAN IF YOU'RE VULNERABLE
SYSTEM INVERSIONS
GOD FORGETS IT ALL
CROSS SETTLES IT ALL
COMPASSION NOT CHUMMINESS
COMPASSION NOT CHUMMINESS
LEARN HOW YOU'RE DIFFERENT
RETIREMENT
I CRINGE LOOKING BACK
EXPERIENCES BRING PERMANENT CHANGE
GOTTA MOVE FORWARD
LIBERAL ENVIRONMENTS
UBIQUITOUS ANXIETY
NARCISSISTIC WITHDRAWAL
COMPLETION
THE WORLD TAKES ADVANTAGE OF GUILT
PSYCHOLOGICAL EFFECTS OF REJECTION
BROKEN BORDERS
IF THEY CAN'T FORGIVE YOU
CYCLES OF REJECTION
THE FAST TO BLAST THE PAST
IT WAS ALL JUST RESEARCH
INGRATES AND INVADERS
ADDICTED AND AFFLICTED
STYLE OVER SUBSTANCE
WIFE OF ALCOHOLIC SYNDROME
ARCHETYPAL FLIP FLOPS

SYSTEM INVERSION

SYSTEM INVERSION

SYSTEM INVERSION

When we swim in muddy waters we get some on us so we're puritans in controlling ourselves.

BULIMIA AND OTHER SYMPTOMS

People get mentally ill as they get physically ill. It's all a reaction to trauma, even narcissism.

It's a Fatal Mental Illness like a moth to the flame, it brings hate and then a double bad fate.

Toxic memories from your mental illness: Put it all in a bag then throw the whole bag out sis.

You were mentally ill due to an early trauma you had no control over so forgive yourself sister.

She wasn't a slut, her mental illness made her promiscuous. What relief, it's joyous.

She wasn't a slut, her mental illness made her loose with men--she had no boundaries man.

It is possible to be promiscuous and not enough know it. Emotionally flat, she just puts up with it.

BOUNDARIES ARE ALL

Spend a year with the Lord in fasting, solitude, prayer then truly see the social world: beware!

They bothered and interrupted me constantly and thus my main focus is setting boundaries.

From mental illness/maudlin insanity to being bubbly in happy gaiety cuz you are well, finally.

The use of force is not attractive but a necessary part of police work or shutting out a curse.

The use of strong assertion laying boundaries brings crafty opposition--no matter hon'.

God put me on earth to be imposed on for years so I'd write about it forever in laughter or tears.

Her reaction to rejection is psychopathic: defiant, reckless, impulsive, aggressive/vindictive.

Her reaction to rejection is the total loss of impulse control: she gets drunk or eats it all.

Her reaction to rejection is to become uglier than he ever saw her before. Repent--turn now!

Their reaction to you laying boundaries is to come anyway. You must be very firm, ok?

Because people will eat up your time, energy, focus, goals and money. Boundaries: every day.

"NO" THE MOST IMPORTANT WORD

That's why NO is the most important word in our vocab. NO opens you up/YES blocks that.

NO opens you up to a world of opportunities based on your talents and destiny, YES wrecks that ok?

NO is like blasting you open to the endless possibilities in just this one day, YES says boring's ok.

SYSTEM INVVERSION

Why let other people write the script for your day? Don't be in reaction, CHOOSE it all, ok?

ALL they did was pressure me to do their thing and ALL I wanted was to stay home: FREE.

So the female though a genius may react to rejection with anti-social conduct--imagine that.

The rejected female genius becomes a psychopath when in intimate settings--the family.

The biggest reaction of wife of the alcoholic is to be the scapegoat and get drunk herself.

Tho' my foes were inferior in every way it was two against one and I caved to triangulation.

TRAUMA BRINGS MORAL COLLAPSE

Moral collapse is a reaction to trauma, don't forget that. It's easy to blame the victim, a slut.

She's trying to close a gap of the original trauma and will do anything to realize that promise.

It was always two against one, I grew up under the gun. Triangulation equals suffocation, no fun.

All thru a series of traumas lasting decades I kept the Creative Act safe, separate--it was my Ace.

The Wife of the Alcoholic Syndrome was so horrible because no one believed me at all.

The wino alcoholic made me the problem and I took that believe system on/was pulled down.

It's Satan in the drinking husband ridiculing her looks and everything else and I was forsook.

13

PRAY AND WAIT FOR ESCAPE

In both cases I outsmarted abusive men by staying silent like everything's ok until the end.

In both cases I escaped by [1] seeing what he was and then [2] praying/waiting for an open gate.

God doesn't want you to be controlled by an abusive man so pray then just wait for an opening.

You know you can't tell him a thing so you stay silent and sweet until that escape opening.

She wasn't suddenly treacherous just secretly waiting for an escape opening my dearest.

I went along with it sweetly for years until I had a chance to report him for all to his peers.

For the truth will come out/MUST come out. You won't be frustrated forever, I promise you that.

FLAT EFFECT [DULL EMOTIONS]

Flat effect [emotionless] in psychopaths: they discuss the most awful things as if it's nothing.

FACTS: narcissism is a post-traumatic condition and workaholism is compensatory/a reaction.

The more you avoid truth to avoid the wrath of narcissist the quieter that voice becomes.

Two-word Bruce has to look at his wife first before he says anything just in case she's pissed.

Men are usually conservative, women liberal. Men should rule not let wives influence at ALL.

SYSTEM INVVERSION

Because dominant wives push husbands to the left our whole country is going down in a ditch.

You're letting your liberal wife--who doesn't know what she's talking about--lead your mind?

First I escaped my peers thru addiction but then in desert solitude I marched to another drum.

They scared me half to death they were so callous. The youth I knew made me homesick.

HAPPY IN SOLITUDE

In desert solitude I was so happy with the elements--sun, stars, sand--but then they'd come.

I hated em they were so callous--I don't see how a mother stands having em in the house.

Movies serve such a human function. Transporting our emotions to another plane then its done.

Since high end producers spend so much time on each frame it's worth it to see a movie many times.

I'm sold on Daily Fasting without dieting. No low lowcarb/highcarb but high quality in daily variety.

If an elder I think you should let go of the past/outer and just look forward to God your Father.

When lowcarb I was hungry for fruit [sugar]. When a fruitarian I wanted fat/salt even butter.

Popular votes be. damned, white house has decided for us: Green Energy's their man.

When looking back don't feel vulnerable but protected by God at the last minute, as it always is.

Narcissists don't care about all that interior stuff. All they need to know is: you're replaceable.

BOUNDARIES FOR ME BUT NOT THEE

They have an inappropriate notion of boundaries. Boundaries are for no one else but "me".

Narcissist blurs your boundaries while their own are impenetrable. Don't allow it/get strong.

For success in love: date smart, break toxic cycles and get the relationship you desire & deserve.

Break toxic cycles, get the relationship you deserve while still being authentic, that's it.

Huge transfers to their guests. Insane pork vague spending bills: it's what they do best.

She couldn't separate her WHO [spirit, child of God, talent] from her DO [demons, errors, sin].

She doesn't know what she's talking about, hasn't read the law and is caving into woke police.

WIFE OF ALCOHOLIC SYNDROME

Alcohol puts us in the left brain and he became a social manipulator with me as the group target.

I would get so flustered I'd dip into his wine and then everyone said I was the alcoholic swine.

Every little mistake I made he'd run with it to the group and peg me as a savage in his daily scoop.

He was so nice when sober but when he resumed his drinking career he was the devil I swear.

SYSTEM INVVERSION

He was never drunk just mildly soused all day, a critical ass while kissing up to the upper class.

Even while suffering I was working all night. I kept it a secret to protect it but now it alights.

I didn't tell anybody cuz they woulda ruined it for me. That's always how it is, pandemic envy.

You gotta work down low with utter devotion in anticipation of later fame and fortune.

The devil tried to obstruct my puritan work habits by people coming over: I had to mature

A crumpled up $100 bill is still worth a hundred dollars. When Jesus erases the crumples, bravo!

LESSONS CAN BE SHOCKING

Luckily God got all the lessons from shock and trauma over when I was younger and stronger.

I had to learn the value of home and never to leave. I appreciate the comforts/pleasant eves.

Instead of making mistakes I'm sitting in a comfortable home thinking about my past mistakes.

I can't believe I was "out there" fighting wars I didn't have to. Home is all, the social eschewed.

Once you see how the cycle keeps you down, just repent/pray to God you'll never do it again.

I can't believe I was "out there" as a pin cushion to their debasements. I'll stay in the basement.

You meet em and they immediately want something. Like Brittney Spears said, a piece of me.

Or you meet em and they immediately insult you now that they can. It's a human jungle man.

I don't want those ravenous wolves in my home again, let alone that Jezebel always wanting in.

Marriage is the only protection for a woman unless she joins a convent, another possible tyrant.

If she makes it past all the clawing, imposing, aggressing and pressuring she's ok then.

POWERLESS POWER PLAYS

It's a power balance of the powerless: the minute she gets an edge she takes over: dangerous.

It's part of the Jezebel archetype to take over when she gets a chance--reject her Dad!

If a powerless woman has it in her mind to dominate, watch out as the tables turn: bad fate.

Knowing how to rule without underhanded means--power--has evolved thru the centuries.

Having no background in handling power when they get it women get mean, ruthless, sour.

Of course I don't mean all women--it's a bell shaped curve--but few make it thru/have nerve.

Who wants a buncha words poured into their brain? That's society and also false religion.

The black sheep eventually leaves the entire system but later he comes back to lead em.

Don't worry over faux pas it was just a blurp in their radar, unless it's all recorded sir.

God said: Let it go, you have limited time to accomplish My aims through you on earth.

She/he's a human dynamo but won't say so. They are low key/modesty--just workin' fellows.

The thing about the help is this: if they can't face facts about themselves they just get mad.

QUEEN MAKES IT PASSED THE BLOCKS

If she can make it passed the blocks she becomes the queen and this is ALL about boundaries.

The Lord has been so good to me of late but back then when in sin He was mad/VERY irate.

The Lord is an EXCITING life full of creativity and with prayer it's almost magic, without strife.

Even at my age they bug me. I feel like many grandparents who hate grandkid's day.

All i want is to live my own life free of interruption and that is being a conservative: free, alone.

The imposing church ladies took great offense when I asked them to stop "bothering" me.

The cross settles it all. We don't need all this chattering and folderol let alone the socials.

Why would the "church ladies" come unannounced to my house anyway? Men rule/stay away!

LIVING WITH A RATTLESNAKE

If too weak to keep boundaries the evil world flows in and like a tsunami--it'll ruin you honey.

It was like putting a rattlesnake in my cage but in my naive victim denial I couldn't see that, ok?

How'd I know this guy--a professional in his field--would turn out to be the devil's tool?

A loved home is a magic home: it attracts what it IS. If they come to enjoy serenity, keep it as is.

How'd I know this. guy--chief of staff--would turn out to be such an ass if I just wanted status?

It's young males causing problems all over the world. Any victim of em is changed for good.

My life was filled with so much violence it pushed me over the edge and now I'm an isolate.

How'd I know this guy--a popular speaker to y'all--would turn out a silly parroting liberal?

THE HIGH CLASS WINO

Get away from me wino, I'm the opposite to you. The mere drop of alcohol = looney tunes.

Wine tasting constantly is your high class escape but I have happy/creative nights and days.

He drank wine from the minute he got up until passing out at night and with you it's all right?

Women swim in muddy waters so past is riddled with sex events: don't go there/just repent.

He got into his groupy fan base with sex events and then we never heard from him again.

Most common murders are black on black, black on Asian, Hispanic, white; then white on white.

According to democrats we're always one tax increase away from prosperity, that's a fact.

If you don't demand respect the teacher will again be a seeker because people are debasers.

When you got freedom from clingers/drip dry hangers they were angry having lost their supply.

The manipulators never cared about your inconvenience, like kids it's all about them.

I had no backbone and they took and took and took with outrageous demands like crooks.

MORE TROUBLE THAN THEY'RE WORTH

As long as they're around you're adapting to THEM. Tell em to shut their mouths/sit down.

As long as you're so involved your own needs are buried under a pile of details--help!

Empaths must guard their inner space and avoid interactions that may wanna dictate.

PTSD is like a constant movie reel, a curse. They're mean if you're weak, that's how it works.

If you're weak you can have fifty imposing on you simultaneously and life is hellish see.

Everyone hates you or is imposing on you: that builds a hard shell and the world can tell.

THEY'RE MEAN IF YOU'RE VULNERABLE

They're mean if you're vulnerable but the minute you're married the persecution stopped you know.

SYSTEM INVVERSION

The minute I got married all my enemies fell into a ditch. Hot coals on their shamed heads.

Underdeveloped empaths easily become doormats for others wanting to achieve an end.

There are three marks of the strong empath: setting boundaries, saying "NO" and self-care.

You're such a strong beacon they see the light and cling on. It's sad but stay detached son.

Tho' suffocated I was compassionate realizing they had NO self/inner reality/God system.

You were the only light they had so they CLUNG ON but don't allow dependency/wean em.

Evil disguises itself as dazzling beauty and unfathomable wisdom but is the opposite of both.

"The way to be happy is to be good". Old saying, anonymous, the way they always thought.

SYSTEM INVERSIONS

If you were the black sheep and sister was the golden child when you repent it's no longer valid.

To fellow black sheep: When you repent the system will reverse with you on top for once.

Being in certain environments lowers self-esteem and changes our view. Get outa there, now.

We see ourselves in relation to others. Like the gangster-priest syndrome, it's all relational etcetera.

The black sheep in the system depends on the golden child as the opposite: they change together.

SYSTEM INVVERSION

When the black sheep becomes the saint the golden child becomes depleted, oddly quaint.

To sinners all doors are closed to opportunity while to the repentant the world is your oyster honey.

When the gangster becomes the priest the priest becomes the gangster or similar.

GOD FORGETS IT ALL

Even women who've had abortions can be forgiven by the Father and He'll give em something higher.

He will give them a Creative Act or something good to give back to the world: God is like that.

A lower middle class liberal town where word gets around that you're not and it's a dangerous knot.

A secret grandiose self longing for due recognition while battling Dunning-Kruger duds all day long.

If interested he'll say but with narcissist's short attention span you may never hear from him again.

Previous eras condoned religious isolation but nowadays you're looked at as a hideous deviation..

Religious isolation puts you at the top but now you're lonely for humans. Stop, look up, trust God.

God gave us cats and dogs for when we're lonely. Persevere, enjoy thy fast, pray constantly.

It's not that I'm lonely for humans but that I can't forget and wanna get back at em. Hmmm....

Cuz I wanted holy separation they found me arrogant like I was above em: a dangerous situation.

God made me peculiar to do His good works despite all around putting me down, the jerks.

Jesus was so exhausted with the masses he escaped to the desert and prayed to the mountain.

CROSS SETTLES IT ALL

The cross settles it all. Not a buncha words and boring meetings after that, that's all we know.

After they preach to the choir--stuff we already know--they start the WOKE crap: it's all liberal.

Best talents really do ripen late. Those are the ones bringing most to God, they're at the gate.

You can't say things have never been this bad. Look at the Holocaust, depression, genocides.

All I know is one thing: Jesus saved me, the cross settles it all. Now, walk tall/it's PERSONAL.

The cross settles it ALL and not one more word need be said but gotta have "meetings" instead.

It doesn't matter if he "understands" or not--you want him OUT! Danger: every minute counts.

After years of fighting for privacy she's finally alone and it's so lonely, that's how it is honey.

WOKE IS: Waging war on those who don't agree with them. It's violent tyranny and bedlam.

The only way I wrote 130 books in ten years is hubby protected me, otherwise it's a fight for privacy.

Even churches wouldn't let me work. They wanted all my focus on meetings/socials: bores.

COMPASSION NOT CHUMMINESS

Like Jesus I feel compassion for them but still can't have em around: this is NOT a contradiction.

My biggest toxic memory is the continuous misjudgment of my identity due to non-conformity.

They're gluttons for fame. Not me, I'm interested in privacy, not being exposed: feeling SAFE.

I can't think of anything more terrifying than fame, I don't understand why they want it, so unsafe.

Development Potential [DP] comes from neuronal over-excitability [OE] and that's me/now I'm free.

I was so over-excitable they wanted to lock me up or call me too sensitive, either way it sucked.

I had to learn about myself, things not taught. Like I hate crowds, have different boundaries, love God.

I had to LEARN how i was different from the others. How my good traits were labeled bad, etcetera.

William James on the saints: they sense SUPERFLUITY in people and it's also true of the ancients.

I had to learn how I was different/how it was misjudged as deficient and it took years accepting it.

LEARN HOW YOU'RE DIFFERENT

Once I learned of my differences the logical end was a house in another state with a locked gate.

I had to LEARN how I hated groups, neighborhoods, get togethers, potlucks and social religions.

There are cultures where all are silent as they go about their work. Hear this you loquacious jerks.

They feel they deserve fame and fortune for being born or looking a certain way. It takes WORK ok?

I had to LEARN never to get in their car or go off with them on a lark, never at the mercy of jerks.

She purposely drove me through toxic paths to test whether I'd get sick, a dangerous twit.

Never get in their car unless you know they're mature and entirely on your side as a darling and dear.

Many men have turned against ALL women. They do things like leave em off to hitchhike home.

Cuz you swam in muddy waters you sinned but are forgiven. You still gotta face it, it's embarrasin'.

Your trauma is no longer outer-based [exogenous] tho' caused by past events. You are now it.

One of the worst things about war if not killed is loss of home--shelter from people, weather, doom.

Since thoughts are things, as you get more refined you will now be better remembered in mind.

Maybe you're not burned out by what you do but the company you keep. People can fatigue.

RETIREMENT

The fact is life has an expiration date and you shouldn't spend it all working-- need to MEDITATE.

As a human gets older it's more inner, not outer. If he doesn't give up the latter he'll falter.

The news whether Fox or Newsmax is REHASH with new views and much repetition too.

When older, use the guiding principal "less is more". Go deep inside, disengage from the outer.

Why waste time with rehashed news that's everchanging too whether red or blue?

I get more from music evoking thoughts than fishing the internet to escape mental drought.

Dirk loved his terraced Southern French villa but when he had to move to London he loved that.

After life persecution Soren's tomb said: "now I sleep in valleys sweet, just with Jesus do I speak".

I CRINGE LOOKING BACK

I cringe looking back. People are pugnacious these days, I coulda been killed: fence up.

I have always and still do dread possession. No one's ever possessed me. Dirk Bogarde

I need someone to talk to but don't talk very much, I get loquacious on airplanes. Dirk Bogarde

A word or phrase can elicit three days of writing, like a string unraveling a sweater to the end.

Retirement should be cozy pajamas: no more adapting to games and the resulting traumas.

What you have to give to the world must be preserved. Stop wasting time too, soon it's all over.

You must find yourself before you die. Spend more time thinking as past pearls are mined.

Not so much useless assiduity or news repetition, retirement is an inner journey/vacation.

Hey, we still have the power of the internet despite their efforts to censor it so cheer up.

EXPERIENCES BRING PERMANENT CHANGE

Dirk Bogarde, my favorite actor: the things he had seen and witnessed changed him for life.

Immaturity is being socially-based. That mean's our reality is not inner, the only adventure left.

Endless details of your physical reality, that's all I hear from you. Let God and prayer enter too.

You don't like the food, you avoid it then cross a line and eat it then you want ONLY it as it all reverses.

You don't want a behavior, you avoid it then cross a line and want ONLY it as everything reverses.

I hear the wind singing through the windows and the windchimes--I'm delirious with Thine.

He's just like most, he just likes the chase. After he's got you you'll be discarded--is this the case?

Wind songs thru windows and chimes outside with sleeping pets inside, I'm in heaven tonite.

Just because someone is old doesn't make them nice/not evil. I had to erase misconceptions too.

An old woman inveterate in her liberal beliefs becomes the most silly/foolish, even a communist.

Just cuz an old woman bakes you cookies and the like doesn't make her helpful/not evil: yikes.

GOTTA MOVE FORWARD

God has touched you with His mercy and grace and now says "go away from the scene of the crime".

Go and sin no more, stop revisiting this, stop bringing this back in mind—just say NO next time.

Move forward with your life and sin no more: a chance to redefine yourself, a great juncture.

You cannot tie self-forgiveness with whether others have forgiven you. That's how the social screws.

Once you forgive yourself the deal is done. God had already forgiven but this is the hard one.

Tho' society tried it, you were never defined by your mistakes but with God REFINED by them.

LIBERAL ENVIRONMENTS

A liberal environment is not an openminded one. Novelty brings scapegoatism and misjudgment.

A liberal environment is dumbed down/rigid and novelty brings negative reactions, that's how it is.

Threshold levels beyond which novelty brings reactions are much narrower with liberals: no thanks.

The narcissist will punish you for not being what they want or thought. I was tied in knots.

Politeness has become so rare it is being misconstrued as blatant flattery or dying for attention.

Trauma is external or originates from within—that's worse since there's no escape, we're the one.

UBIQUITOUS ANXIETY

Worst: all-permeating, ubiquitous anxiety and depression from endogenous [inner] mental illness.

There are no outer correlates to the trauma, it's all inner-based tho' events can trigger mental illness.

The exogenous--the outer--is obvious when it comes to trauma but the inner is for a psychiatrist.

This is it: I'm in total safety right now but the brain is constantly reliving 35 years ago when not.

For depression/anxiety that is soaring, excruciating, imminent: we develop coping strategies.

Don't worry how they had you pegged, the New You will floor em/make old archetypes of non-effect.

They won't be able to see the old you and the new you at the same time--the old will cancel, aye.

Coping strategies [for inner trauma] are: Personality Disorders. I was a nut case & life was a bummer.

Personality disorders like contumacy regulate and ameliorate feelings of trauma from treachery.

A total psychopath doing insane and deviant things is controlling the inner events happening.

The narcissist self-sufficiently withdraws from other people: he is a self-contained ego-system.

NARCISSISTIC WITHDRAWAL

The narcissist is unable to bond due to a lack of empathy and pervasive sense of grandiosity.

Due to betrayal trauma she lost all boundaries and morals and did insane things, very out of control.

SYSTEM INVVERSION

The false [made up] self of the narcissist is the driving force of his personality, as with schizoids.

Narcissistic contempt and a sense of superiority: when combined with immaturity it's jail-time see.

Tho' withdrawal has an arrogant/oppositional quality it's a secret grandiose self longing for recognition.

Social isolation was condoned not condemned in previous eras: fast forty days in the desert.

COMPLETION

You've been forgiven for all the terrible sins bringing on these curses which won't be ever again.

Every single time they came they brought their evil army against me, the flying monkey frenemies.

God doesn't want us to be scared all the time. He also wants us to love ourselves/get into line.

Completion attracts pollination. You're finally done so attract the link to success and you've won.

Stop reliving the past the overcoming of which brought you here, your reward for coming thru it.

Just cuz he pokes at you after breakup doesn't mean he wants you or finally has a relationship skill set.   .

Someone can leave you and also miss you at the same time. Don't think relationship/not his style.

After completion, work to stop writing. It's a compulsion but now it's blocking new cycles starting.

I'm leaving the earth soon so I hope you take these words to heart. Be holy separate, be apart.

It's a grey cloud invasion of mediocrity, a tidal wave giving me a headache--all I want is escape!

Now that you're complete, wait to be discovered. Your completion will attract pollination for sure.

COMPLETION IS TWO-FOLD

Completion is two fold: completing your work and forgiving your self no matter what.

You can't go forward without self-forgiveness. It's not selfish for the future is blocked with less.

Since He forgave you, by not forgiving yourself you're out of synchrony with destiny/nothing works out.

Self-forgiveness was the missing key for me. I held a grudge against myself for my humanity.

Anything can happen when Satan's in control and everything did. Put it ALL in a bag to go out.

He was tortured/died for sins to be erased so to continue to hate yourself with shame is sacrilege.

It's all about selfies & events but WHAT have they done? It's just a run around, fools all of em.

Unforgiveness of your self blocks the anointing--God doing thru you what only He can do.

As a psychologist I know what self-hate, self-disgust, shame and guilt does to a person/it sux.

They act like they're rich and famous just cuz they were born, not having to do anything for it.

Toxic religion confuses being saved with being a doormat. Nothing is more false but I believed that.

Why do we love people who don't love us back? We're snared by rejection, that's the #1 fact.

Instead of saying what a great writer you are why not just write and let them decide you are.

They brought you down/wasted your years but it was only due to sins of yours that that occurred.

God said "I forgave you for all that". It doesn't matter what humans think as they gossip/chat.

THE WORLD TAKES ADVANTAGE OF GUILT

The world always takes advantage of one stuck in a pit of guilt from things done/bad choices made.

Unending guilt is trauma/bondage. How long will you feel it? Self-forgiveness should be immediate.

God the Creator and Almighty makes provision for our bad choices since that is being human.

Wherever sin abounds grace does more abound so He's given us the means to cover the unsound.

Mistakes make grace necessary and the growth coming out of it is the intention of the grace.

God provides a way out of turmoil even when it's self-inflicted, a way back to balance In a mInute.

The appearance fades, the body bloats or disfigures, appetites compensate emotional torture.

Rejection is like a virus which depletes the soul of all the antibodies necessary to fight rejection off.

PSYCHOLOGICAL EFFECTS OF REJECTION

Rejection leaves us longing for the very thing that is killing us as a void is created of emptiness.

As the mind, will and emotions are totally depleted the rejection itself becomes as an addiction.

When the soul is deficient rejection becomes addictive: yet another painful irony in psychology.

A deficient soul is out of sync with God--unaware of His unique value let alone a godly lifestyle too.

When one has not been loved and nurtured completely there's a void screaming to be filled.

That void is the Deficient Soul, bringing a desperate desire to have that area filled: whole.

The void dims the holy spirit--discernment--so he/she gives all love to the next one to walk up.

The goal is desperate: to fill void immediately if not sooner and it doesn't matter who's the sucker.

To fill the void is a matter of psychic survival, to repair the original trauma bond with mom, a rival.

I was filled with these complexes so went out to the desert to solve it and just depend on God.

At first I was desperately lonely but it all dissolved to reveal the absolute: just me and Almighty..

It was then I realized I was loneliest in a crowd, and I'd felt that way since Kindergarten, awkward.

BROKEN BORDERS

When lonely I got involved with who everyone warned me against with earnest and I settled for less.

SYSTEM INVVERSION

In total desert solitude with just a bicycle I felt God suddenly and the tedious world fell away.

I've been in total solitude ever since and it's been thirty years of bliss--not a people person I guess.

That's after years of going after men & on the begging end--a fish swimming upstream, drowning.

The more they'd reject the more I'd chase because I had a trauma bond with mom to solve.

A woman should never chase a man--to do so is unChristian--but trauma brings desperation.

No Christian love in the home = desperate trauma bonds and voids filled with low-lifes and scum.

IF THEY CAN'T FORGIVE YOU

If the family SYSTEM can't forgive you, let em go. Don't get addicted to changing em, it's a whole.

The lost soul invests all in the next person indiscriminately: "I can love you into loving me".

As the relationship turns toxic the victim can't tell the difference between normal/abusive.

The rejection breaks the soul to the point that there is no more discernment of what is good or bad.

Right or wrong, proper or improper, decent or indecent, refined vs. gross--all lines break down.

The void was so great I was a people worshipper. But in solitude with God it all fell away. quickly.

When rejection and abuse becomes the norm distinctions are lost of proper vs. improper.

Rejection is like a drug becoming an addiction: an ironic attraction to the most harmful person.

CYCLES OF REJECTION

When one's already been rejected when it happens again it becomes a toxic bond seeking union.

The rejection addict says: I don't even want this but somehow I keep reaching for it and need it to live."

"I can't pull away from it. In the back of my mind I'm thinking this is all I'm worth/all I deserve."

Rejection bruises ego, compelling victim to return for validation and to change the perception.

It's what happens when you've not developed in the things of God and go along with the crowd.

Potential suitors can be lined up around the block but you want the one that rejected you to accept you.

You don't seek the validation of God. In your mind you want the one who did the crime to love thine.

You're seeking the only thing to bring closure: finally them affirming you and nothing else sir.

THE FAST TO BLAST THE PAST

I always knew before success I'd have to fast and 96 hours seemed the best to past the test.

Don't treat the fast lightly. Don't watch the hours go by just enjoy a divinely rich time with Almighty.

To not-eat is a test of character and the knights. It's the last one, a phantasmagoria of true delights.

SYSTEM INVVERSION

Don't underestimate the fast, prepare for visitation. Now's the time you make hay while glowin'

All disease is obstruction, all recovery elimination, all success attraction cuz now you're fastin'

Don't long for the time when you can eat again, enjoy this special time when the great mind expands.

I filled my mind with loved movies and characters like friends and redefined/started again.

IT WAS ALL JUST RESEARCH

What I went thru was hell but worth it to write these books about crazy people & the social.

I learned by trial and error about people. Not thru psychology books but by being fooled.

In my four day fast I watched my four beloved movies simultaneously, alternating and thinking.

Altho' I've seen em a hundred times I always gather new insights seeing em again while fasting.

It's a technique I use to expand consciousness while fasting, like a ten-fold increase in fidelity.

With favorite gorgeous/deep actors, the fast combines to redefine identity but it's you see.

Transcend all humans. At some point you gotta let em all go anyway, we leave the earth alone.

Paul took it as his first priority to forget whatever is past and step into the future God had for him.

It was hard for me leaving the horrible past since I live in my head so what else did I have?

The boys wouldn't leave me alone and the police stood down. That's the blue states on the coasts.

INGRATES AND INVADERS

It seemed to me the whole younger generation was like that: imposing, lurching, invasive, tyrannical.

I kept saying "I'm not interested" and they'd react "why not come with us?" It was outrageous.

They acted like they owned me, like I didn't have a right to not be interested, a subhuman feeling.

It's not happening today since an older woman is usually behind a locked gate/not a victim of fate.

It's no different than gestapo knocking to extricate me--it was worse than the wild west, truly.

That's Borrego Springs in a blue state where kids take over small towns and cops stand down.

I'd lived a sheltered life in a conservative Christian home and was thrown to the wolves all alone.

The town was totally liberal. Everyone I got involved with took me down a rabbit hole/awful ordeal.

They were grasping, lurching, asking for things. The communist spirit as taught in the schools.

I couldn't wait to get away from them--high school '85. They were arrogant/presumptuous/thieves.

Women were cruelest always colluding about one usually--opening gossiping and calling it Al Anon.

We don't even need cops where I am now. Everyone minds their own business in their homes.

It's our actions determining rewards or punishments. Live a happy life by getting that thru your head.

ADDICTED AND AFFLICTED

I was wrong, in error, addicted. Life hit back hard and I was afflicted. Now I'm free, a happy kid.

I wanted to eat everything in sight, drink every last drop, listen to loud music and turn it up.

It was like a bottomless pit inside, a deep dark cavern into a collective unconscious, a sad lonely ride.

The biggest thing man must conquer is not other lands but HIMSELF. Taming the instincts is all.

Saying "I'm not interested" is apparently offensive since it puts you first as a free will expressive.

The therapy was to be ASSERTIVE in laying BOUNDARIES and that took a lifetime of enduring misery.

The minute I got married the bedlam stopped. A single girl has a bull's eye painted on her mom.

I'm not gonna get involved with someone if the result is mental illness being in their system.

One wrong involvement and decades go by in a painful blur. See the light, God wants you happier.

It makes me mentally ill to witness what you're into and to meet your brood. Desert rats rule.

I'm at the point where I don't waste one minute. With full amplitude in mind I keep expanding it.

STYLE OVER SUBSTANCE

With the left it's always style over substance. That's how they operate and what gets their attention.

You didn't have the boundaries laid and firm since you were addicted with no boldness: infirm.

I know how important self-forgiveness is so by you pushing my face in the mud, forget it.

Saints sense superfluity in the herd. There is no subtlety or refinement just polite cruelties.

WIFE OF ALCOHOLIC SYNDROME

Jimmy was a cuckhold, he never would protect me. In fact he handed me over to the enemy.

He'd changed so drastically with alcohol the bottom fell out of my reality cuz to me he was ALL.

Via alcohol he'd aged thirty years overnight yet emotionally had regressed/not a knight.

From a kingly archetype he's an old ogre suddenly, someone I didn't know/want to know really.

From this lower archetype he targeted me and linked with the ladies against me, always gossiping.

He never would of gossiped from his kingly position from before--he was above all that, but now...

ARCHETYPAL FLIP FLOPS

With an archetypal switch the spouse is thrown into confusion, panic/isolation/identity destruction.

The minute he resumed his drinking career with me as target Satan couldn't have been happier.

SYSTEM INVVERSION

How do I know you won't turn on me also? That's how we get after a war without solution ya' know.

Gossiping like old women at the well--that's how he seemed to me now, hardly a king to look up to.

As things regressed interactionally it affected my appearance, giving him more to pick on.

I entered the vice grip when the others joined in against me. The alcoholic must do this apparently.

Wife of alcoholic syndrome is like a snake wrapping around until you're dead or can't move again.

JOLLY JIMMY TO THE WORLD

He was jolly Jimmy to the world but a sadist to his wife--thus I was seen as the savage in our life.

He cozies up to people [alcohol's a social lubricant] while the wife is always angry with the drunk.

My stint as wife of an alcoholic was a war without end, even when he was sweet it was tentative.

Alcoholic: serial disappointments, broken promises, games of dominance, shame/guilt so toxic.

I kept trying to get my Jimmy back--what happened to him? But there is no going back, amen.

The alcoholic feels guilt and shame, a result of the allergy, which is projected onto the family.

God uses the experience of every mistake you make to make you the man/woman you are today.

What the devil uses to define me in a pit of guilt God uses the RE-FIND me. Self-forgive = best version.

SELF-FORGIVENESS: THE LAST KEY

The herd can't look beyond certain things but God looked beyond all of em forgiving me.

You don't have to campaign for votes, those supposed to be in your life will see that you're the most.

Forgiving myself simultaneously unleashed the faith I needed for the future God had promised.

Once you've forgiven yourself you can't worry about another's reaction, it's dead now man.

Once you forgive yourself it unleashes a positive expectation for a better situation.

One you move past your past you automatically develop faith for your future, just imagine that.

You can't get others to believe in you until you self-forgive, otherwise bad energy hates the self.

Reward: the anointing is the presence of God to produce through you what only God can produce too.

Count on God's presence to break the shackles of guilt and shame to step into that anointed place.

Everything is crushed when coupling the forgiveness of the father and the forgiveness of self.

CALUMNY

Sister Sins: Calumny is the deliberate, malicious, untruthful accusation injuring a neighbor.

Idle but mischievous chatter is equally looked down on in most religions, though it is not slander.

Many have fallen by edge of sword but not so many as have fallen by the tongue. Eccl 12-26

Bearing false witness: In descriptions of a corrupt society, calumny is always the most emphasized.

"They bend their tongues like bows for lies, all walketh with slanders"--sounds like Borrego Springs.

Calumny so deserved special and severe punishment the rabbis saw leprosy as its just reward.

Living wrong, holes in your bucket. Live right, God rewards with prosperity/what you want.

Being resentful over the past shows ingratitude for the present, your reward for coming thru it all.

I've done stuff like that myself. Get desperate, pull at straws and make up wild stories of hell.

LETTING THAT ERA GO

When I let resentments over previous eras go a whole new dimension opened up all aglow.

I saw the benefit of released energy, cuz life is like a pie. It goes here or there and I felt a tornado inside.

I then saw to finish these books also, to release even more energy for new directions: WOW.

I saw that less is more--less assiduity meant more insights gained from just sitting and thinking.

I've done the work assigned to me but everything has completion--to be really done at last.

The more I release old patterns the deeper my thoughts are going--release, release, do even more.

End completion of 130 books, no more editing or refining but really tie it up in a knot/don't go back, finish.

What will I do with all this excess energy after completion? Look out the window, thinkin'.

Before marriage I was always explaining myself but once one man understood there's no need at all.

Leave psychology and take up painting or maybe just answer questions or enjoy every minute.

To be truly done with your life's work AND the miserable past opens up a new artistic world so vast.

DEEPEST OCEAN

God puts old sins in the deepest part of the ocean with a sign which reads: "don't go fishing".

Not so heavily conceptual, not always exploding contradictions but just enjoying divine minutes.

What does psychology mean in eternity? I'm leaving the world of interactions behind re: treachery.

Insight: To self-forgive is to stop writing about psychology, now isn't that a revelation.

I wanna be like Frank Lloyd Wright/Picasso who did their best work in their 90's then suddenly died.

I'm sorry if you can't forgive me but I must forgive me to go to my destiny so that is how it will be.

I'm supposed to forgive myself--that was the one key I was missing. All this time, reminiscing/remorsing.

To be resentful over the past is to not appreciate the present reward for coming thru it--stop it.

What is a Kellockialism? Brutal reversals and the resolution to all contradiction in a cute little poem.

The weaker they are the more they rely on flying monkeys to their dirty work--against YOU, God's first.

They're all so familial while you sit here on the TOP of a hill, no one questioning you/need to explain yourself.

It's the gossiping weak females who are most reliant on flying monkeys like the sheriff is their sidekick.

PTSD AND SIBLING RIVALRY

Having great Scottish pride, the hateful accusations and calumny of my sisters created PTSD as I cried.

It was literally like I was being hit with an axe every time I heard what they said, created and embellished.

PTSD can be from war or the internal wars in families thru history where ONE is the victim of other siblings.

A triangulation of two against one [a constellation which never changes] is a template keeping one down.

I was a sensitive sheltered child and sibling rivalries shut me down, turned me off, kept me frail/sickly.

What they did and said about me I could not believe. It shocked my nervous system/put me in PTSD.

ATTACHMENT INJURIES TAKE ODD FORMS

I now see it as an attachment injury with my mother dating to infancy and taking very odd forms truly. S

It's the MOST sensitive, gentle, intelligent and even exalted beings who are most hurt by attachment injuries.

With the early trauma the exalted being **REVERSES** into one mean thing: enantiodromia, flip-flopping.

When sweetest becomes meanest that's what I'm talking about: enantiodromia, personality inversion.

Successful genius eventually finds **ONE** he can rely on while letting others go--now he's ready to show.

Finding **ONE** you can rely on is a placeholder since things always change but it's perfect for now.

The bible says we'll always have **ONE** good friend and I always have though going into solitude again.

I hated people thinking life was all like this. How would I know it's because they were liberals/feminists?

These were disgusting women/creepy, clingy dependent men. So ungodly when I compare to back when.

Look at WWII docs to see what the general public looked like--like movie stars, decent and refined.

They all asked: **HOW** could a genius have gone so low? Well it's a matter of a **SPIRIT** from below.

Creepy losers drop in all the time, having nothing better to do and using you as a pit stop too.

Borrego was hot and liberal. YUK! I learned more than a library of books about psychology, abnormal.

Borrego was great when Republican upper middle class but liberal children took over: death, run by asses.

A TOWN RULED THRU GOSSIP

Borrego run thru grapevine where women ruled thru gossip and cops visited Liquor Store Linda for it.

SYSTEM INVVERSION

Borrego was hot/surrounded by mountains squeezing us in together--you'd see an enemy daily or whatever.

It's a catastrophic/appalling fall from grace, suddenly. Depedestalization is also very embare-assing.

What can I say, you're now dead. You did yourself in by arrogantly talking like that/showing us hell.

What can I say, you're dead. You did yourself in by arrogant overreach: The Fallen Hero Syndrome.

You see, my words are like atom bomb. You're not just on pause--gonna have to build back up again.

You have to go back on the Potter's Wheel--who are you? You've been living a lie/need time to heal.

I loved you but that was a delusion--I didn't know who you were and part of me was into self-destruction.

Sex is sacred but to you it's as mundane as going to the bathroom feeling superior in your words/actions.

The old boy's club, huh? Feeling superior as you talk against women/make sacred sex mundane.

Well you've fallen in my eyes now, it's embarrassing and I won't be back--we're now fully **NO CONTACT**.

If you think I'd put my divine stuff on your cheesy channel you got another thing comin', goodbye now.

You were the one with the pure spirit, putting up with all kinds of abuse for it and praying daily for a let up.

ARISTOCRATIC NEATNESS

Neatness is a sign of good character so bring some order or I'll be done with ya cuz chaos is torture.

It would be like teaching a pit viper the values of love. Get over foolish notions you can change wolves.

Of course I don't like coming into your orbit. I'm a neat nick and can't stand the disorder or seeing it.

Suddenly I can't go in either of my two cars. Chemical sensitivity is progressive/I'll stay home forever.

I've been carsick all my life. Dizzy, bilious, nauseous, acidic, can't sit up, coma--little gas chambers.

You turned me away as you seem to be interested in sex for sex sake and not true love--a big mistake.

You talk too much about sex man. Not just a player but an old player--time to get a new gig much higher.

Who wants to conger you thrashing about in bed with some anonymous broad? Shut up you sot.

It's really disgusting as it became the fashion to gross us out with sex passions better hidden.

If sex isn't sacred and hidden with restraint then it's not sacred at all but common as dirt as man falls.

War is boy's favorite game then videos take youth the rest of the way so is violence any wonder today?

LET DEPEDESTALIZATION OCCUR NOW

His depedestalization has finally occurred. Suddenly he's gone from consciousness as an annoying curse.

Self-confidence is great but why subject yourself to ridicule? Let your work stand on its own you fool.

Why argue with Whoopie types of liberal feminists? Don't bother with em for you're way above this.

SYSTEM INVVERSION

Why go on national TV like The View to be falsely accused while they call your leader a liar? Stay alone/higher.

Being a triple Pisces the devil had a MOST terrible effect see? Enantiodromia are OPPOSITES in thee.

You are either the best or worst. That's the glitch that must be overcome: rising affluent prince or bum?

People are either thrilled by your very appearance of DISGUSTED, turning away from a sick dunce.

Because if you don't have it--if God's removed the fire--there's nothing you can do to renew it.

God removed my fire once and I fell flat on my face. A public disgrace: the humbling of an ace.

God gives you charisma or he can remove it all, making you an ordinary, inconsequential Neanderthal.

You sin past that line for the last time and the spirit ceases to strive and now you're living in a bee hive.

For one's secret sins WILL be shouted from the rooftops eventually--things always come out sweetie.

Stuck in their ego, people assume it's THEM and their power will always sustain--no way, it leaks away.

These are the things I've experienced. Exhilarating UPS and heartbreaking DOWNS all which I own.

FAMILIES WEAPONIZE HISTORY

Weaponizing history: This occurs in families so to get well geographic relocation is a must to grow/be free.

My past: "I'm scared of all of you people. The world is a drought, I'm appalled, all I see is cold hearted evil".

49

SYSTEM INVVERSION

My real education was a Ph.D. in the Streets from what I learned living in liberal town Borrego Springs.

We were all pushed in together encircled by mts in a hot desert and couldn't escape the gossiper.

A town can morph from high-class republicans to low life liberals in one generation, that's what happened.

They would come to my cabin and demand in--they have no respect for property rights nor privacy.

The architecture is anachronistic from the 80s for social: no fences and the front door's on the street.

I wouldn't be social and it was an affront to y'all and some of you even got violent before your fall.

People constantly knocking on my door/calling on the phone. Now none: a gate ensures home fun.

Borrego's another blue town where cops won't protect you from thugs--the ACLU won't permit it. Huh?

They won't arrest teens breaking down your door or smashing your windows-- the ACLU you know.

They wouldn't arrest my tormenters just me for one beer on my moped-- everything was reversed dad.

For a woman the only way to live is to STAY HOME and be married for PROTECTION--life within walls.

JUST NEED ONE TO LOVE YOU

Get ONE man to love/marry you then he protects you from all OTHER men out to get you--its historical.

Life was only resistance like a fish swimming upstream drowning but marriage changed everything.

SYSTEM INVVERSION

Forget the social and get ONE to love you then that greases the skids/everything goes ok now.

But feminists see marriage as bondage, when it's total freedom for a woman if properly managed.

You must find a spouse who will protect you and your cats for our pets are most precious/they love us.

If you're still doing that it's an unrepented sin and caution: God' will pop your balloon in a moment son.

Never let anyone in your house unless you're certain they love your pets. I've had terrible accidents.

You can be so enamored with someone and then suddenly he makes you sick! Knowing this is a neat trick.

A late bloomer blossoms on their schedule and the best talents ripen late: endure insults until out the gate.

Father, I know I was to blame but now it seems way too late tho' You can change everything the bible said.

If you can grow up and get past all this crap I'm still interested but hanging by a thread, get it?

GETTING THE HELL OUTA DODGE

I thank God He led me outa California 5 years now. Things are so stable here I feel I'm in a dream somehow.

There are demons over streets, families, towns, regions & nations when sick thinking infects everyone.

Getting the hell outa Dodge, man--that's what it's all about. Geographic relocation then hold your head up.

PTSD: Intrusive thoughts and avoidance of going out. Don't wanna see anyone and memories hurt alot.

PTSD: Sleep deprivation/anger issues triggering adrenalin over and again--it's a big deal friend.

Beauty is SYMMETRY and the ability to push thru harsh environmental factors while maintaining it.

If weak we may react to stressful environments by going lopsided: pushed out on one side: uglified.

The stress was so great I could only adapt by going into desert solitude in a little cabin on 1000 acres.

Millions of strong/handsome young men were hopeful and happy then slaughtered in war, think of that.

Some were most likely to succeed having grand plans then were wiped out like they never lived.

THEY'RE DEAD BUT PTSD REMAINS

And here they were torturing live animals in their science labs but being rich they were beloved as-is.

They're dead and gone now but the PTSD remains. Isolation is my way of life now, it's a GAIN.

I remember being in painful stress for months/years. Even soldiers get R and R but there was no let up ever.

I was invaded by a gang of boys as the cops stood down. If weak, PTSD attracts more trouble all around.

The Cinderella template of two older angry sisters was repeated with other women keeping me down.

These women were so ruthless and sadistic I felt hit from all sides and my universe seemed to collapse.

The lady said "my two older sisters betrayed me in the Cinderella Syndrome/I was sick till they died".

Thought loops: the trapped thought without a date-stamp causes intrusive adrenalin-triggering shocks.

I don't even know who I am. The PTSD caused severe depersonalization so I avoid interviews ma'am.

Forget interviews, I don't wanna be seen. That's part of PTSD for the key to survival is SECRECY.

Satan uses our own instincts against us. He'll do it again cuz mentally the sinner can't cover all bases.

PTSD brings depersonalization. You don't know who you are, invisibility is survival, won't even see your photo.

TOXIC SHAME BY SICK SYSTEMS

Toxic shame hooks you to sick systems where you're treated like crap. You accept blame, that's it.

After being gang raped the horrified woman shook in rage and fear for months--the bad effects are much.

That demonic dyad was like a steel trap: two feminists always colluding, gossiping and loving all that.

They think you have more than them, now you're a target. Must go low key to fight this communist spirit.

Why open a pandora's box to be open to ridicule just to sell books. The link WILL come to you, rely on God.

A sick family system can put one through a personal war spanning decades, so strategically relocate.

TOXIC SHAME means you feel unworthy. One feels heaviness, an abyss, nothingness, defectiveness.

I felt like I was not enough. Like I could not do it. That I needed someone. But that was not the Truth.

How to deal with Toxic Shame: Understand that it's there and how it overcomes you in a shame spiral.

In a shame spiral, become your parent telling you the TRUTH about who you are, discounting the other.

At this exact point you see the shame as something OUTSIDE of you, not sweet as a dove you.

Toxic shame indicates somewhere there's an abusive parent and later you probably chose that.

The lady said "just when I'm happy with myself a shame spiral starts and my mind goes dark/anxious."

FAMILY MYTH: NOT GOOD ENOUGH

Somehow a family myth came through to me that I wasn't good enough and deserved to be mistreated.

But when you have toxic shame that's how you'll allow people to treat you-- and here we go again.

That's why we become people-pleasers: to silence these voices of shame saying we're not good enough.

Common myths: How you think/feel is not enough, your worth is not enough, your work is not enough.

Waves of disapproval wash over us constantly in an unhealthy family and there's no reinventing.

You don't have a spirit to go out and create in life's game due to a victim mentality steeped in shame.

Avoidance attachment style is associated with this shame that prevents bonding or even gaze fixating.

You analyze for years WHY your husband has the malady and after all that study he still has it honey.

With so much stress the personality fractured and now he's only defined by routines, likes and dislikes.

Jesus cleansed it all making it white as snow but due to PTSD bad memories keep cycling thru ya' know.

It won't work so why try? But then the other party is thinking: this will work, can't wait, why delay?

When I was targeted by a gang of boys and cops wouldn't protect me, PTSD became part of my personality.

RECOVERY FROM INVASION/IMPOSITION

It's not something you can easily recover from. There's no pulling yourself up when memories keep you down.

Those "boys" are in their fifties likely with no thoughts of what they did to me or my feelings of safety.

This was in the 80's--their kids are the ones about to throw Molotov Cocktails into your homes soon.

Once they found out cops stood down they could do anything/come anytime--I lost all privacy/liberty.

Who wouldn't be afraid of youth who seem to have no lines, like there's nothing they wouldn't do.

I've just always preferred being alone. No one's company do I enjoy as much as my own.

CHOOSE IMPACT NOT FAME

It's not that I wanna be famous but I want to get my point across. Be kind to children/animals please.

Somehow talking about the evils of the past makes you the bane of the present. Greg Gutfeld

Beauty is the strength to go thru disaster maintaining symmetry and I've done that you see.

My own sisters, my God! It's like the profundity of a Greek tragedy which is always about family.

Since identity is relational, the desire to keep the upstart DOWN is the way she stays grounded.

This last book is on boundaries and borders because that was my whole problem: INTERLOPERS.

That inner cry, that rage--tho' it's all been assuaged and you're finally safe it still remains.

Tho' Jesus has already set us free we feel bound with insecurity from our abusive history.

I felt like I belonged nowhere and wanted to die. I was a stranger in a strange land I sighed.

GETTING DRUNK

It's no excuse that you did such a dastardly act while drunk! It's no excuse, but it's neurologically explained.

With the mere atom of alcohol in the system the brain changes and the devil works thru us, amen.

The prisons are full of murderers who killed while drunk. it really wasn't them: "in vino veritas" is false.

As a triple Pisces I don't dare drink, even Nyquil. Because another being takes over and it's total hell.

They asked why you did such a terrible thing and you said "I was drunk" but that didn't matter bud.

The point here is not to drink at all cuz the world won't excuse what you do when you [CHEMICALLY] fall.

IT'S A *CHEMICAL* SWITCH

They used to say how you act while drunk is the **REAL YOU** but I'm saying it's the opposite: it's the **NOT-you**.

It was so horrible waking up in the morning to what I had done or said! It was so ego-shattering I had to drink again.

It's been 26 years without a drop and as I continue to clear up I can't believe the danger I was in, unable to stop.

It's a moral desensitizer, leading to the most degrading things leading to more drinking just to cope with memory.

If you have jealous friends they'll make you worse while drunk than you've ever been. They'll encourage sin.

They soak you dry, rape you and take your money too. It's the Fallen Hero Syndrome in the life of all alcoholics.

A young drinker will later have to go back and emotionally mature thru all the phases/he missed the basics.

The most basic thing like **BOUNDARIES**--which all animals have--I had to learn being open/without resolve.

ALCOHOLISM: NO HEDGE OF PROTECTION

Sin breaks down the hedge of protection and that's why I let them in: it's entirely predictable, so repent.

As long as I was in sin I had to adapt to people--be controlled by them some way and to put up with evil.

I also had no self-defense--which every animal has--and thus I was a sitting duck for users, losers and dunces.

Having repented of major sins I sit in protection and no one ever bothers me. What a difference, believe me.

It's as if our sins release an army of demons and then envy and calumny are coming from all directions.

It's not that what you do while drunk is YOU but that you OPEN UP to devious demons below, a slew.

You don't stay captain of your own ship when drinking. But you always THINK you are--that's the thing.

ANOSOGNOSIA

Alcohol is an instantaneous SWITCH from right to left and I don't ever wanna lose that artistic gift.

Take a couple beers and I can control the outcome. That's the recurrent thought before your psychotic shock.

What else can happen when everything already has? When Satan takes the reins it's worse than outlandish.

Satan is so devious and he WAITS. This has gotta be a hard and fast rule: don't drink but a little herb is ok.

Alcohol brings on ANOSOGNOSIA: loss of pattern recognition and making an ass outa yourself hon'.

Anosognosia means you're killing yourself without the ability to see [PATTERNS] that you're killing yourself.

Anosognosia means you've left the cornucopia of the right brain and are now in the grey linearity of the left.

It wasn't a small liberal town it was a den of jackals and thieves--what lessons I learned in my teens!

FEMALE GENIUSE ISOLATES

Mom was a genius [built our homes] but an isolate. Out of protection of dignity/smarts she just stayed inside.

Much of your shame is trauma-based. It helps to know this, since it's more mechanical then your mistake.

Unplug, reboot, restart, return to factory settings. That's why I fast 72 hours on weekends and recommend it.

The past was like a nightmare: it educated you but now that you know, let it go--God wants it gone like a vapor.

For love, build trust. Trust is built when our words conform to our actions. What we say we do = I love you.

With lack of trust we think they're gonna cheat. Bad behavior follows and home is a war zone, not sweet.

Everything I say he copies then acts like it came from him. Just an example of empty narcissism.

THE CULPRIT SAYS HE'S THE VICTIM

The narcissist will use your reaction to his abuse as proof that he is the victim of you--he tells everyone the scoop.

Narc Scheme: he abuses and provokes until you rise up, then he calls you crazy, abusive and unstable.

Even if you don't justifiably react he'll find something you did to make HIM the victim of YOU/you're screwed.

He'll find something you did to justify the abuse he's heaping on while showing himself as YOUR victim.

Lady said "I went decades thinking I was the problem and he was the victim, allowing him to make all decisions".

And thus his narcissistic injury from long ago is compensated for, you're down on the floor and he's superior.

They abuse/degrade others in order to emotionally regulate themselves and from that comes family wars

With acceptance that they're the victim of you, they're empowered and the false self is back too.

GO NO-CONTACT OR GREY ROCK

In receiving wrath/scorn from a narcissist family member, stay low and stoic or most desirably go no-contact.

Staying low is also called GREY ROCK. That's the only way because getting re-ensnared is dangerous/sux.

"Narcissistic supply" is ATTENTION making them feel special and superior. Watch them change, oh my.

Their abuse is never ok. Learn to read their patterns with our primary slogan "observe but don't absorb."

Narcissist fragmentation: He is this, then he's that. He's not changeable, he's ALL of it but it's unconnected.

If he's a narcissist he's changing constantly and doesn't apologize for anything, he's just himself see?

You shouldn't want someone who's so changing/never saying sorry cuz you have enough on your plate honey.

AVOID THE SOCIAL FELLOWS

Sorry I'd rather be a nerd into complex theories than a social climber in intricate networks and hierarchies.

I'm just not into all those names and fames like you are. It's intimidating to me, I'm into the elements/stars.

So you go back to your outer world stuff and I'll happily retreat into my inner reality I've built up.

I feel like I'm competing with the whole world with you. It's too much, I will resume my happy life with few.

SYSTEM INVVERSION

We're into two separate life phases. I want detachment and solitude and you want it all meaning I'm screwed.

Goodbye, I wish you success, happiness and many friends while I resume my inner journey to The End.

I don't want what you want so I can't waste another minute. Using reason not my heart I now reject all of it.

I'm interested in science theories/sound doctrine and you're just flipping around socializing all over town.

That's what I get for wishful thinking. An impossibility but desire stepped in when I shoulda been praying.

I woulda been good for you but you're so into people I just have to withdraw. Quiet, peace, solitude, God.

It appears to be a cult of personality and so sorry, I'm not in the peanut gallery. I want science not the silly.

It's not that I'm shy, you were just the last speedbump before final completion and crossing the Great Divide.

CHILDREN OF ALCOHOLICS

I was brought up by a borderline: raging alcoholic, angry woman and a Jekyll and Hyde.

I felt unseen, unheard, ignored, not liked, not validated and extremely scared of her.

It wasn't her it was the booze but still the effects lasted for years in the symptoms of a fool.

My two older sisters became liberal feminists of hate and a whole new dimension entered the gate.

They were so bad, nasty and catty I realized my mother wasn't a problem at all really.

My scary mother ceased being a problem when I became her drinking buddy, that's my story.

IT'S CALLED SYSTEMS THEORY

The intricacies of these complicated systems affect all members and it means addiction/depression.

Not being seen, heard or understood: do I even exist? That's the beginning, then the twist:

My life as a known entity didn't even start until Jesus rescued/restored me as His sweetheart.

Mom had an abusive drunk father--it's all passed down. I saw it this way to stay grounded.

This is a story about going from a NOBODY to a child of God: this is called INVERSION or flip flop.

System Inversion is where the bottom becomes the top/the top the bottom as the devil got him.

ENANTIODROMIA: EVERYTHING REVERSES

You can be held down for years and in a twinkling of an eye be at the top-- that's how God works.

System Inversion is called ENANTIODROMIA: everything converting to it's opposite.

Become the opposite: we must hang onto that. The bible recounts reversals: to saint from brat.

With attachment injury, however, we get STUCK: attracted to jerks who keep us in the mud.

You can be rejected by someone and feel like a crumb for decades, a lowdown bum.

SYSTEM INVVERSION

With attachment injury already coded, the rejection leaks into it and we're the bottom of the pit.

The rejector goes forward looking for new supply but you're dejected and for years may cry.

You fail so return to the original system which derailed and now you're slow as a snail.

So that's the system: it passes down, it copies and reduplicates, it maintains bad traits.

BORDERLINE FLIP-FLOPS AND DUAL PERSONALITY

At one point I was suicidal and wanted to be dead then I'd jump for joy and dance instead.

Dad was docile and wouldn't protect me from her, a harridan the whole neighborhood feared.

I loved my father the best tho' with both I made peace before their death, but these feelings persist.

It took decades to realize I wasn't BAD as my sisters said and then I didn't want to be dead.

The bad image they pegged me with acted as a computer program to fulfill it/act it out.

That's a person without unique personality innards--he takes on the image given by his superiors.

DOUBLE FOR YOUR TROUBLE

In Isiah I read God would give us DOUBLE reward for former trouble--it was like it solved a puzzle.

Life wasn't so horribly unfair after all. Everything comes around to the beginning with God.

It's not just stories of others lives, it can happen to you if you're willing to believe in the Highest.

It was hard to crawl back up since they'd pegged me as terrible, a criminal, a no-account runt.

They planted evil seeds against me so everyone else would think like that: that I was bad.

Evil feminists are the worst gossips and they'll ruin your reputation when they're the bosses.

If they're jealous of you they'll join with envious others and now it's a crowd of haters.

These people are too needy to be independent they'll always group with others--believe it.

Misjudged, I knew they'd never understand and I only escaped thru marriage to a REAL man.

MARRIAGE IS A WONDERFUL SOLUTION

The solution for protection for a woman is to marry a REAL man and make a REAL go of that.

Not a beta male who is so weak he'll slide in with the enemy or minimize the social tragedy.

If anything happened to husband I'd still be ok cuz at least now I have a WALL to keep em away.

I repeated: "If God can do anything for anybody then God can do something for me".

Before the problem even happens God's got a way to turn it around--He's always got the solution.

Even if you feel He's forgotten you, God hears you and has a plan for your breakthrough.

ADAPTING TO FEMALE TYRANTS AND WITCHES

I saw how feminists think ANYONE is bad if they don't agree with them and it's very sad.

This isn't harmless, people's lives are derailed by feminists in the family who are ridiculous.

If we learn something from the mistakes we make it gives us character which shows on the face.

Who can deny they grew spiritually from all the hard things they overcame in life, truthfully?

RESTORATION GIVES BACK WHAT YOU LOST

The biblical definition of RESTORATION is: to receive back more than you lost, amen!

For Christians the final state is better than original condition--faith is rewarded/we're quickened.

I'm a better person cuza what I went thru in childhood and later when overcoming it.

Without all that it would just be a theory in my head rather than gut-wrenching experience instead.

One of the reasons God lets us go thru all this is to equip and qualify us to be in His service.

Your catty family--the sick system--can come back in your head and the day is ruined instead.

The devil thought he was winning but actually he equipped me to help others thru writing.

Bible hope is: a positive expectation that something good's about to happen any moment.

It's not so much they're "bad" but they give in to their default setting to do the wrong thing.

When you get old don't wear clothes for a 12 year old but also quit saying "I'm too old".

How many people are hurt by their siblings and never get over it? Millions, we can't even guess it.

They misjudge you, tell you what you ARE then gossip to legitimate all their slander.

They get you in a box you may never get out of, or escape to do your thing to be proud of.

It's the SYSTEM that's predominant and that means it's mostly the siblings stepping into it.

I was the ground defining them until I grew up then their world was shaken/they had to block it.

IDENTITY STRUGGLES AS GROUNDS CHANGE

We define ourselves against the ground of others so when they change we feel disordered.

Tho' you were unwanted and unnamed, don't park at the point of your pain, step up again.

Life threw me under the bus too but I decided to drive it. Joyce Meyer

If you went thru parent/sibling pain like that, God is the only One who can pay you back.

Some suffer their whole lives feeling unwanted being adopted--the emptiness of feeling unbonded.

Marriage was the first time I felt understood in a cold cruel world--that's how you should feel girls.

Because people are cruel and they will use you, and any friend can become dominant too.

I was ground defining them until I grew up, then their world was shaken/they felt they were falling.

THE PIE IS LIKE A BUDGET

It's a SYSTEM and it's like a budget. More here, less there. Change this, the others are pist.

I'm sorry you went thru it cuz discovering your reality was a FAKE is hard to take but now, make it.

God promises to heal and restore--so don't go by your feelings but look forward to much more.

Tho' they call you an outcast it doesn't matter cuz God called you peculiar-- His brightest.

Tho' father/mother have forsaken me the Lord will adopt me as His own child. Psa 27: 10

Only completion attracts pollination of this great and marvelous work and wonder, meaning MON.

I'll just call em Cinderella's Sisters then it won't be like I'm gossiping about those bossy losers.

It was hell on earth so I can truly relate to husbands and boys having to put up with her.

FROM ENDEARING TO VIRTUE SIGNALING

SIMPLY BY accepting the liberal democrat line you automatically and already know they're swine.

For how could she possibly go along with that crap? And she's your wife/sister? Give me a break.

And then when she gets power her tyrannical and illogical control creates hell's worst hour.

When women lose the humility making them tender and endearing it's just ego and virtue signaling.

Females: from sweet and tender to virtue-signaling and angry--some even seem like killers.

Be very grateful that you have access to God because these people are so far gone.

IT'S NOT ABOUT A DRESS

It's not about a guy wearing a dress but pedophiles wanting to rape your children sis.

Intrusive Thoughts. Do what I do: when California comes thru I mentally explode it too.

We're spoiled brats forgetting the freedom we have but Hong Kong values it, imagine that.

One thing you must realize is that they KNOW. You think they don't but it's an aura from below.

What you should do is what you do effortlessly all day long anyway cuz it's what you do, ok?

You can bring good stuff thru or bad. I brought bad thru for years but now I hope it's all good.

I can see why momma didn't like you Dave, Chuck, Danny, Rick, Costa, Jimmy and Shane.

It wasn't you I wanted [you nondescript fool] it was to solve the original family system drama.

BOUNDARIES

Having no boundaries and imposed on constantly I felt ANGER and that became my power.

ANGER is the godly force behind setting boundaries and asserting them IMMEDIATELY.

The child of dysfunction can't set boundaries, he's adapted to being a blank slate for sillies.

The social generation can't set boundaries, they've been taught that the social is all there is.

Before I set boundaries life was pure torture. How'd I know it was a generation of losers/lechers?

Living without boundaries is so dangerous its a wonder I'm alive but God was with us.

ANGER ORGANIZES EXPERIENCE

If you feel anger, you've been harmed--so look around and discern what happened.

It was not ok as a child to feel anger so it always felt misplaced and worse, it became generalized.

I was being imposed on, interrupted, stopped, blocked, censured, slandered, redirected.

Anger used creatively ORGANIZES experience so you set INSTANT boundaries naturally.

I can honestly say these troubles made me much more able to keep us safe, fruitful, stable.

I had to pretend I was happy and never complain about the bad things: Pseudo-Mutuality.

I wasn't taught ANGER was normal or there to protect me--only to be dishonored in me.

When your soul is being murdered it's natural to feel anger at the injustice--oh, I've been there!

Being disconnected from anger and unable to show it made it easier for exploiters to move in.

Anger turned in to depression and suicide thoughts. That's what happens as the brain rots.

Inward-turned anger affects your appearance and even makes it look like a rabid mental illness.

The child will do anything to keep parents happy like dissociating from or "swallowing" the anger.

As the rage builds up you have a personality that is angry ALL the time and doesn't know it.

ANGER HELD IN WILL DRIBBLE OUT

I kept seeking nurturance from the betrayal source and that explains my entire neuroses.

ANGER also results in passive-aggressiveness: gossip, do sadistic things, creating messes.

Anger finally rests on the victim mentality--a buncha anger that's so exploited it's become silly.

As an adult you need anger to guide you, set boundaries and protect your rights.

People are cruel, they will impose and take cuz it's not the fifties and now you need boundaries.

Recap: know your rights as a human being and get in touch with feelings: ANGER predominantly.

Victimhood is unintegrated anger which blocks understanding and thus boundary making.

SYSTEM INVVERSION

Not respecting who you are, breaking boundaries, betraying trust/cheating, abusing physically.

Someone who doesn't make you feel good/makes you feel bad, takes your energy away.

They bring their friends or impose on you right away but then you're a minority and don't say.

LETTING ABUSERS BACK IN

Letting abusers back into your life is very dangerous for your soul and brings a terrible fall.

Why is this: You'll leak self-esteem and feel you don't exist, which you don't being boundaryless.

Internal boundaries are a MUST keeping you from seeking nurturance from betrayal sources.

Tho' parent didn't know they weren't giving us love we needed, it's still betrayal/that life ended.

The child has no one but the parent so to please it he will deny his own needs and NOT EXIST.

ABUSIVE BONDS FOR SURVIVAL

It's totally sick to yearn for an abuser but common as dirt in this generation of bad parents/losers.

The CHILD: For survival he even must BOND with the person being abusive towards him.

Since he needs parent to survive he must bond with the betrayal source and that's the conflict.

Yearning for someone who betrays you wouldn't feel right if your upbringing was healthy/loving.

Longing for the betrayal source? Are you kidding? That's what a healthy person would be asking.

They're rude and mean and blow up then calm down and be all-nice again: that's abuse man.

ABUSERS: People who exploit or bust boundaries while they assault, steal and rise up.

Mean and nice all day: what this does is cause an addiction to form/cycles without end, OK?

Harmers--in any way--should never be allowed back in your home/get restraining orders today.

Once you can SEE them for what they really are--commoners everywhere--you are a STAR.

Then the most important thing to do is relocate and for sure get a fence and a locked gate.

See what's going on to take adequate measures to protect your heart and treasures.

Letting an abuser into our crib is like letting someone in with a knife to tear us up: please GET THIS.

INTERLOPERS: WOULDA BEEN OK ALONE

Perpetrators who cross boundaries, are exploitative and abusive can never give real nurturance.

Like I didn't have a right to privacy or boundaries and was hateful for even wanting it, really.

Jezebel can't smell danger [cuz she IS it] therefore never take her advice or it's soul murder.

Jezebel spirit will ruin your life until she or you is dead--crying "peace", out comes wrath instead.

Let a disrespector back in life and it's all downhill from there because your message is clear.

Taking an abuser back is a self-batter but with early betrayal bonding it doesn't even matter.

I couldn't see any of this. I had to be run in the mud for years until finally no more Mrs. Hostess.

What empowers the perpetrator is Betrayal Blindness resulting from attachment trauma.

If that's all you know early, as an adult you don't feel the abuse until the next day when you're angry.

Constant deep level emotional pain from this disrespect then being put down again.

CRITICAL PARENT MAINTAINS RELATIONSHIP

Your critical parent keeps you down by causing tolerance/longing for abusers you've known.

Your wholeness and independence causes you to be aghast at the thought living without a FENCE.

We yearn for abuser-nurturance he had originally--he doesn't come as the devil right away.

Perpetrators come nice, bearing gifts/good news, flattering, couldn't be more enthused.

If you're choosing someone who's hurt you in the past, it's you who is two-faced, wrong, all gas.

No liberal can BE THERE or be your friend due to their tolerance/preoccupation with sensual sins.

For sensual sins will always come first while anything else important becomes far worst.

And you addicted to a loser degrades everything around the same way, so go away.

When I saw him again I couldn't believe Elmer Fudd was the source of my addiction, even a friend.

The crap he liked/his music seemed so PUERILE like he hadn't grown at all when it came to STYLE.

When I finally found desert solitude alone the chaos was gone: pure perception full-blown.

I unpeeled the onion back year by year and eventually came to a child much happier.

MAKE YOU LISTEN

The awful part about feminists is how they "make you listen" and it's always so unnerving/boring.

They make you listen having a narcissistic idea about themselves--like they're equal to Trump.

Why grace her with his presence if she won't do business? Save yourself the trip Miss.

If he won't 100% agree to the feminist narrative she makes him listen till he escapes to relatives.

Why would anyone self-deflate like that so suddenly? It's due to an EARLY trauma and injury.

As I come to the finish line I feel exhilarated like the ocean is running through my veins--Ole!

Why would anyone self-deflate/wreck their career? Cuza other people then or now, my dear.

Liberals don't wanna re-win the debate over gays or abortion but will have to cuz we're not giving in.

SYSTEM INVVERSION

SYSTEM INVERSIONS [ENANTIODROMIA]

The **TABLES HAVE TURNED**. The bottom has now become the top and I'm ready and armed.

SYSTEM INVERSIONS: Enantiodromia [book 100]--the biggest reason is they just die off.

She spat all over me one time--how'd you think that made me feel? Mothers aren't saints, they're real.

She didn't even like me--recognizing that at forty started a **WHOLE** new life of work and joy.

As I got weaker (2 against 1) she went on the side of my sisters and the betrayal made me crazier.

SEE THE SYSTEM

It's a **SYSTEM** as we ricochet, join forces, build a worldview, connect with allies, separate.

The queen is shrewd as she slyly balances forces around her and it's a constant thing for sure.

Women fight and compete socially and it's cruel as hell. I'm sure you've been there, please tell.

When it comes to the System women rule everyone and if she's a feminist you will be ruined.

It's no small thing ruling family and home--that's the whole thing, the **SYSTEM** until we're old.

I've arrived at the notion that the more I divorce from this the more success is possible doing less.

That inner cry, that rage--tho' it's all been assuaged and you're finally safe it still remains.

Forgive yourself for anger and rage cuz much of it is an introject swallowed in another age.

Videos are cruel so people become cruel. Already weakened by systems they tolerate evil.

See it: he's a horrible man and a snake. Take off that loving image of his, he's really a fake.

I carried you along all my life and now I see it was an empty vision/delusion, trauma at the beginning.

I look at you now and can't believe it. I longed for you all my life and you sure weren't worth it.

EFFECTS OF SIN

You dip into sin and you will lose YOUR way again and come under the control of foes or kin.

The abusers are dead or gone now so this is really about human nature vs. individual growth.

it's PATTERNS in human interactional systems coded into nervous systems and later making messes.

Pack your suitcase and forgive yourself for everything and anything, it was just a script.

Don't worry it's just an attachment injury I carry around with me--it's not about Steve.

When it suits their ends they trivialize everything. It was a LIE not just a "misunderstanding".

No man on earth would hit a decent woman--these women are abusive. Jesse Lee Peterson

Most women don't tell the truth about what THEY DID to get the abuse.

SYSTEM INVVERSION

When one gets well another gets sick or he gets sick again. Homeostasis: That's systems theory.

They enjoy cruelty cuz it takes em over the edge-- otherwise they'd be bored stiff instead.

With the death of the family everything becomes a silly game as they do crazy things for fame.

HIX POLITIX

Socialists like AOC don't care about the price tag it's just a BIG promise to the Millennials, sad.

They get elected, they get power and they run the government. Look at Detroit, amen?

What they call "socialism" is really globalist crony fascism on a deadly depop mission.

They point to trashy blue cities as proof we need socialism when it's the left doing it all to em.

ANTIFA is a leftist enforcement arm made up of angry teenagers and SJ Warriors.

Homelessness is the moral and political crisis of our time and it's spiraling along with crime.

Any Jew who'd vote for a democrat shows either total ignorance or great disloyalty. Trump

The reason Cultural Marxism won't last: it allies with Islam which goes against it's values fast.

THE NEW GREEN ARISTOCRACY

The New Green Aristocracy like Meghan Markle is blatant hypocrisy and a real tragedy.

She has a Hollywood idea of how princesses behave--an irony of Magan who's all the rave.

The irony is Meghan is a bigger snob than the royals there for centuries--the "woke" royal pretty.

Rashida Talib used grandmother as a pawn to draw attention to her hatred of Izrael and Trump.

Women are master manipulators--give em a little power and they'll ALWAYS take over.

The coalition between left and Islam will fall apart on it's own identity politics as Islam predominates.

LEFTIST CONTRADICTIONS

For the left will defend LBGT rights until it succumbs to Islam which always predominates.

Hatred of Trump will hold the left-Islam coalition together until it doesn't, then watch out.

Making America the bad guy is all the same crap--why is everyone coming here then?

The left tries to silence conservatives by making them cultural/social/family outcasts.

But as mean as they are in ostracizing us it may push many more into the arms of Donald Trump.

History and government in our schools is not just poorly taught but irresponsibly politicized.

Capitalism is evil and we're a nation of oppressors: These are the ideas of commie professors.

SIN MAKES US UGLY AND OLD

You think you're cute? You can be ugly suddenly when God's beautiful light is removed.

That's why the green tree flourishes but is then mowed down like dead grass.

That's one way God gets you back. He can restore your youth or make you ugly/old too.

Even the cutest get lines and boxy looks after 30, just imagine with sin in the works, oh my.

Sin not only makes you ugly it gives you a muddy aura not a beautiful one like heroes in history.

To look right you must BE right or you'll look lopsided, irregular, ordinary/not spectacular.

Sensual sins take the top of your head right off. Now you look more primitive, a low IQ chump.

ROSY POSITIVITY IS A BLACK CLOUD

It's how sin works: The rosy rainbow of positivity becomes a black cloud of total misery.

And there's no way to control it cuz it's a budget: you rob energy that way and you LOOK it.

Whatever you do don't sin before a public speech or anything else if you're trying to impress.

Three days fish, four days fruit smoothie and having both in the day is way too much.

Macadamia nuts: something so delicious and fatty to eat and it's so easy, that's a must.

What to do with a skinny wrinkled shriveled: fast it and it all goes out together, believe it.

I love the 95% rayon or cotton it's the 5% spandex that's rotten and should be verboten.

KISSING THINGS GOODBYE

If you're gonna reach your destiny you must learn to kiss things goodbye/walk away gently.

God'll move people out of your life who were ordained for the past, not the future, so byebye:

Narcissist reactions to correction: silent treatment, stonewalling, gaslighting, blame-shifting.

A narcissist hates you having boundaries for how dare you have needs of your own or allergies.

A narcissist doesn't see you as a separate person with needs of your own, you are OWNED.

People in your life may just be SEASONAL and will leave as the seasons change, that's all.

As they leave, don't hold on esp. to a betrayal bond. Here's your test, pass it to move to your crest.

How you handle the closing doors is key. Don't bring bitterness into the new season—be a gentleman/lady.

NO MORE CHIP ON SHOULDER IN FUTURE

Having a chip on your shoulder belongs in the past–with God's new things it cannot coexist.

You won't have strength to move forward weeping about the past, it takes too much out of us.

Reliving hurts and thinking about past is consuming and life is a budget–sapped, you'll be losing.

SYSTEM INVVERSION

If someone left you, I say this respectfully: YOU DON'T NEED THEM, stop your hankering.

You've spent enough energy on the past--that doesn't take you anywhere but less.

That door didn't close by accident, God is directing your steps--He's got someone better than your ex.

Just as God opens doors He closes doors and this can be hard, feeling like a setback or war.

Quit reliving mistakes made--when you kiss the past goodbye you're released from feeling betrayed.

God is Alpha and Omega--beginning and end. The END is more exciting than when things begin.

ALL ENDINGS BEGIN NEW

So don't freak out when God ENDS things, it's the best possible set up for your future as king.

You can't be what you're created for with a chip on your shoulder wrecking your glorious future.

I know, I was angry at past people too--and it robbed the necessary energy to proceed/accrue.

The pain of the past is such a block I recommend you see the PAST as payment for reward NOW.

I went through all that pain to learn the lesson I couldn't any other way, to give it to you today.

It was horrible not having boundaries because as a baby it was always them imposing on me.

I became a blank slate for other's projections--tho' anger went deep I voiced no objections.

The strength to say "NO" or "leave me alone" was not in me, this blank slate became willy-nilly.

BORDERS and boundaries: There's nothing more important for our nation or you and me.

Democrats are the party of anti-Jewish, anti-Izrael and anti-white radicals. President Trump

I experienced this, I was ruined by the things people said. Social manipulation is brutal and sad.

NO CONTACT!

BORDERS: For it's contact = CONQUEST. You don't even wanna see em at the door, no more.

I had accepted his gaslighting that I was nuts. When I saw the narcissism I was able to release the klutz.

Within a week of going NO-CONTACT friends and family start coming back: fact.

In the idealization phase your confidence goes up but in devaluation phase he brings you down.

They're now not juvenile delinquents but "young persons impacted by the justice system."

No criminal is reformed by pretending he's not a criminal by renaming his crime as minimal.

WE NEED CIVICS

You can vote your way into socialism but will have to fight your way out of it to freedom.

We need CIVICS in the schools cuz kids don't know a thing about government and it's so dangerous!

SYSTEM INVVERSION

Which is why they go for AOC--dangerously false dogmas sound SO good to the naive.

Ilhan Omar shows the feminist arrogance of making us listen to her boring and insulting words.

The poor congressmen having to sit through the slow, deliberate, beside-the-point words.

Most of us can't stand to hear the voices of these nasty stupid upstarts who've taken over.

They know they're all over media so they're playing it up [STYLE] to the dumbed down kids.

We need CIVICS to keep our liberties which are dangerously threatened by brats, kiddies.

These people are so shallow all they think about is food or sex--sensual addictions and appetites.

Times in history where this kinda crap took over and men's minds were trapped in tyranny.

For only thru morality and repentance can one have the vision of freedom and the hell of losing it.

But if you don't have knowledge of how our brilliant government design works, we will lose it.

You know they stink to you so just be a saint and be way above the herd who thinks its superior.

BIDEN CRISIS

It's open treason to put 65 million people who wanna come here in hotels, but he would.

This is how they abuse us: by continually expanding what the word means "extremist".

The new movies are about sadistic Mexican cartels or homosexuals male and female.

The new movies are making us fear Mexicans and have ultra-respect for gays and lesbians.

There is no crisis, but the crisis is Trump's fault: Biden narrative on the southern border.

They want an invasion/America's collapse cuz then the only answer is to become communists.

By US code, the Biden administration is committing open treason against this country.

Disorder: They're not "Latinio" if they're against illegal immigration and open borders?

They're pushing "Asian hate" to get them to be democrats and join the other victims ok.

ELECTORAL COLLEGE AND AOC

AOC types don't wanna persuade middle America, they wanna dictate from population centers.

America isn't majority rule--we are a republic, we have states rights and have electoral college.

The deride the electoral college as immoral when in truth it's most moral, protecting the rural.

Without the electoral college, California and New York would be running the rest of us.

If they're RUDE, say it--how can you answer a question that's more of an impertinent accusation?

Instead of working on self they adopt pseudo-moralistic stances to look good to others.

It's the opposite of compassion to put children in the hands of smugglers but the left's ok with it.

Both coasts are creepy. The affluent conformists on the east/debauched fascism on the west.

Abandon the electoral college and there is no more common man just an elite-controlled mob.

AFFLUENT COASTAL LIBERALS FEEL SUPERIOR

The affluent liberals on the east coast are wall-protected while we gotta put up with it.

The affluent liberals on the west coast are gangsters and don't care about the homeless sir.

Most coastal liberals work for big corps that demand conformity to all that modern crap of course.

They want open borders yet live way out in gated communities where no immigrant is.

They wanna be with their own kind, we wanna be with our own kind but that's racist, oh my...

"Illegal" is not a race. Stop acting like this is a race issue and we'll save America too.

The frame you by asking accusatory, inflaming questions which peg you at low levels.

WE'RE ALL SINNERS AND MUST REPENT

We're all sinners and we all must repent. WE all have a sinful history we'd like to forget!

I am not at all pharisaic. I hate religious tradition and legalism. It's not about the law but repentance is central.

My dad didn't berate me for my wrongs, he showed me what was right—that's mercy alright.

God is the Father running to his son who had blown it then refusing to remember any of it.

The forgiving father didn't dwell on the past but put a party together after thinking his son was lost.

I had a voracious appetite. These things are demons--now I hardly eat anything.

Gluttony is a SIN. Youtube celebrates gluttony in mukbangs: talking about sex and eatin'

GLUTTONY AND GROSSNESS IS TAKING OVER

Grossness has taken over as something good, expected or celebrated--it's everywhere.

People used to be refined but that's relaxed more each generation and wow-- what a decline.

Gluttony and sex talk: that's the modern muckbang highest earners and boy are they rakin it in.

When I think of how I wanted to eat the whole universe--it's a demon I'm rid of.

I do best on baby food. In blender put: frozen mangos or strawberries, collagen, superherbs.

Digestion is just too expensive in energy terms, also pain like acid reflux--it's an obstruction now, I like blenders.

Fruit, cream and nutbutters are utterly digestible. But so much else sits there and causes problems too.

FRUITARIAN BY DEFAULT

Fruits are my food be default. Everything else, without fail, causes problems or makes me a nut.

I've tried the starches--grains and nightshades like spuds--and they poked holes in my gut.

It's not a matter of bragging you're a fruitarian. It's your last effort to save life from daily mayhem.

You say you're fruitarian but still stuck in the taste trip. You just haven't learned your lesson yet.

When hunger attacks after beginning a fast just persevere through it and it won't persist.

In order to heal the body don't give it any more food to work on. Let the energy go to healing hon'

Even if fasting hurts it's fun to know you're finally progressing from the muck/being stuck.

To endure the hurt of the fast means you're FINALLY making gains as the old debris is blasted.

So endure it--forget the fruit smoothies today. Go all the way cuz you know God wants it that way.

In hurt is gain. That's absolutely the thing you remember when in pain as all units are reassembling.

I just don't wanna eat cuz I'd rather make hay: make moves towards healing, more than OK.

THOUGHTS ON PURITANISM

Processed bakery tastes good but eight hours later you wanna die. You will pay for eating this way.

Or unstrict attitudes about sex--these are demons we want rid of, Puritanism is efficient.

People hate moralists--why? Because mankind loves it's sins it hates the preacher guy.

Right is right and wrong is wrong but they can't see that, they wanna relabel everything.

Gluttony mukbangs coupled with the most deviant sex talk I've ever thought nor heard: high earn.

Anyone who can hold to their morals amidst these muddy waters is super-sexy to us, really.

You must actively resist these people and their constant moral undertow, stand up now.

For it's not funny it's downright disgusting and severely destructive to our destiny.

I used to swim in muddy waters, I took it on. I didn't even know it until I matured far later on.

If the most productive time is looking out the window, do more of it. Muse, dream, think.

Be like Brad Pitt: NEVER read your reviews even if it's for twenty years, what do you care.

GET THE RIGHT PERSPECTIVE

America began as a CHRISTIAN nation and we follow the bible which calls it an ABOMINATION.

Learn about WWII where millions were killed. See what life's really about to stop complaining over nil.

Get the right perspective: Watch WWII docs on the most destructive war in the history of mankind.

Doesn't it depress you? YES but it's the right perspective--we're living in la=la land, naive/unprotected.

SYSTEM INVVERSION

I've studied **WWII** history and believe me what you worry and talk about is meaningless gibberish honey.

ORGANIZED COLLAPSE OF THE WEST

Organized collapse of the west: no wealth/free choice but vertical consolidated integration for technocracy.

Citizens have never been more at risk from dangerous policies by their own locally elected officials.

Minneapolis tells residents: obey criminals prepared to be robbed and these very politicians are loved.

Standard cultural Marxist move weaponizing history: saying whites always massacring minorities.

"Whites have long history of vigilante violence against minorities"--false, we just wanna live/be free.

"Whites are killing minorities" is the **STANDARD LINE** of these fascistic revolutionaries--commies.

Why I watch **WWII** documentaries hon' is because we owe it to many millions to know what happened.

If many millions were killed 80 years ago it can happen again and your normalcy bias is naive friend.

Socialism is a brand that reinvents itself in every new naive generation. Greg Gutfeld

We're to banish our whiteness seen in these characteristics: perfectionism, sense of urgency, getting 'er dun.

What marks whiteness? "Perfectionism, objectivity and individualism" so now they'll be soon gone.

Even the monkeys are putting on masks under peer pressure and it's the same for us, yes sir.

White supremacy: It's our success that proves it to them and if we say we're not, we ARE.

Caveat: The NAME of the bill has nothing to do with what's actually in it, it may be the opposite.

DIETARY EXCURSIONS

This book series should be called a psych theory plus my travels through all diets, experimenting.

Lunch with little, sup with less. Better yet, go to bed supperless. Benjamin Franklin

Oligiphagous: superior species exist on fewest varieties. How about grapes & scampi?

Feel so much better now. Fruit smoothies in the morning then later a little starch or protein which is secondary.

The very "white" foods they put down--sugar, rice, popcorn--are those with lowest glycation.

Low glycation makes you look like an angel man cuz there's no wrinkles from fat/sugar cross linkage: gladness.

Perfect day with no acid burn or pain. Mango smoothie, popcorn and fresh apple juice rest of the day.

They act like "fiber" is everything but you can't just do it--you must personalize it or suffer for it.

FIBER HELL, KEEP IT SMALL

Doing it the way "they" say meant I had a big mass of fiber in me and HELL to pay for three tortured days.

Fiber doesn't cure cancer it just makes a big pile of poop making you think it's the right-on answer.

SYSTEM INVVERSION

FIBER theory is a menace: a bowl of nails in your stomach and even with the thought I'm in pain with it.

Go easy on fiber theory, personalize it to fit your tummy and watch it carefully/note things honey.

A little bit of organic jasmine rice, fine. But to huge bowls of raw salads and fibrous starches, goodbye.

The dangers of pasting their diet into your life can be lethal so I behoove you to test it all/make it personal.

By deleting fat you must eat more to get calories and that is the problem: fiber's all that's left unfortunately.

Proclamation: I never felt better in my life. Mango Smoothie, popcorn, apple juice, ole.

They found corn's a fruit. No wonder I love it so much, it's the one starch I can take for lunch.

If you're not hungry, don't eat. That's me after corn, I'm satisfied for 1-2 days, that's the elite.

GLYCATION IS MY CONCERN

People got way healthier in the depression with no food! Eating less, or fasting, is God's simple tool.

GLYCATION: The further I get from oils, animal, processed or fats of ANY kind the more elated I'm getting.

Popcorn or fruit, the body doesn't care where it gets it's necessary glucose. It's not like vegan tyrants.

Glycation is AGING but foods with near-zero glycation are most demonized: WHITE sugar, popcorn, rice.

Low glycation: Fruits veg grains tubers. High glycation: avocado fats nuts dairy meats processed

Go ahead and eat your bloody meats with 9000 glycation and I'll stick to white rice even with sugar on it.

It's simple conditioning: I don't throw apple, cow moos. If I throw more apples he knows moos work.

A fruitarian has such a highly developed sense of taste the slightest mildew etc. and that's it.

ARTS OF PALEO FASTING

I felt embarrassed/ashamed to be alive. Even normal human functions made me self-despise.

It was overpowering. I woulda done anything for my fix at the moment. It was demonic.

After scampi I can fast three days. Protein does it: paleo-fasting is great. Shrimp or grapes?

All that starch encrusted and mucked up the works. I'd go paleo--just fruit, nut, veg, animal.

"Soft" rice noodles are still a grain filled with lectins resulting in excruciating pain, oh man.

Superior species are oligiphagous: live on fewest varieties, that's me I guess: grapes/shrimp.

In diet, "constantly bringing balance" means constantly reversing from what you had last.

Reversal dieting/meal rotation is so the problems of one food or group aren't compounded.

In this life phase I don't do well on fiber. Even if it's soft rice noodles it feels like a bowl a nails I swear.

The frozen grapes, piece cheese and scampi diet suits me perfectly cuz it's easy/I can't think.

THE END OF 130 BOOKS ON SOCIAL SCIENCE

I pray God turns off the spout so I can retire but if He wants me to I'll continue to spout off.

I finished the 112th book--will now dissolve into eternity with only relation the bank and me.

I don't even want to get the news let alone defend my words against them, I'm past all that too.

Ten more pages and I'm done with the 130 books, my greatest achievement on the earth.

I hope you get something out of it, even if just one of the 40,000 quips of a new psych theory.

Finish this then I couldn't care less I'll just escape back to the wilderness and peacefulness.

I've done my work for the Lord and THAT is my greatest reward: Peculiar but Adored.

This is COMPLETION of a structure in nature. Handle it like a crate of eggs, that is mature.

130 books on a new social science took ten years but behind that are decades of work and tears.

COMPLETION IN NATURE

Can't wait to get off this ship/give birth to the 44 yr. old Creative Act I always had to put first.

9 more pages and I pray Lord You turn off the spout if not just for a little while so I may regroup?

It'll be done by or during the weekend. I'm not gonna rush this thing called COMPLETION.

9 more pages and God will turn off the spigot and I'll finally have a life INDEPENDENT of it.

This is a definite milestone coming up. 130 books on Social Science and it's complete, I'm done.

To all you sisters/brothers who said it couldn't be done, I proved it could and will now reap--what fun.

I wanna go into music and the right brain now, not so much verbal tho' this verse is of a higher order.

I'm so used to people arguing with me--I've had a lifetime full of it. I've done my work, enjoy it.

LIMIT PROPERTY GUESTS

Ok you can hook up but no friends/family here and no knocking on my door to charge your phone.

I gave one a hookup without power and they spent their time in my cabin completely taking over.

I'll let warriors like Jordan and Ben go out there and do battle, I've done my part and just want home and hearth now.

I speak to those who read my words--the "copy". I won't appear other than that, why should I?

Finally, after maturing underground for years the holy sage becomes visible to the whole world.

Five cats. who think it's their house and I'm just mom and it's all ok, it's a cornucopia of love.

Back then men were so handsome with shiny hair and tall and thin/not like today's boxy specimens.

Back then men were impeccably dressed and neat, not like today's disheveled mess in jeans.

We love our cats--don't you dare put down our love of cats/say our homes smell like a cat box.

COMPLETION ATTRACTS POLLINATION

I can control and edit a sentence but not an interview and I'm not into that/I want it PERFECT

Be careful with fame cuz increased visibility is the likelihood of attack/you can't take that.

After being in a creative environment entering a socially fascistic one was traumatic/hellish.

The problem is their guidelines are murky yet they reserve the right to ban you anyway.

Remember, it's the inside of your mind we wish to evoke, not a buncha details, a yoke.

We wish to trigger our inner revelations, not having silly ideas and details crammed down.

Prostitutes make money, writers make none--unless they prostitute themselves writing bunk.

The Creative Act is an actual structure in nature with a beginning and an END, then pollination.

So, after all these decades it finally became visible on the earth plane and I was off to the races.

Your COMPLETION attracts POLLINATION. It's pure synchronicity and a soul in transition.

Is it shyness or waiting for God? I tend to think the latter, and He will supply me that minute He wants me loud.

Unplanned videos can go very wrong with poor character. I'm into perfect frames, one after another.

I can't stop the writing just cuz I want to. It's up to God, I wish He'd give me a vacation soon too.

When I came outa the desert I was marching to a different drummer like a different culture.

An older woman behind a locked gate in a safe state: that's my reward for overcoming bad fate.

The thing about the help is this: if they can't face facts about themselves they just get mad.

If you think about it, if God has forgiven everything what do you care if mere mortals haven't?

When I woke up I was scared to death about what coulda happened. But it didn't--God stopped it, amen.

It was a nightmare living in the land of Dunning Kruger unable to explain myself to the losers.

To have to write books to justify yourself so they won't lock you up--imagine such a predicament.

PET SHELTERS

Any shelter for homeless pets becomes a euthanasia operation otherwise you'd have millions.

The thing I hate is "no kill shelters" cuz it means a loved pet goes into a cage after owner's death.

A delirious writer stoned on good stuff and cats all around stoned on catnip: what a life.

Leave this world, go right into the arms of Jesus. Not afraid of death just the care of my pets.

It took me a day to do simple mental task I'd done a thousand times. Time to retire from rhymes.

100 KAREN KELLOCK BOOKS

AFFINITY OR MISERY
AGELESS CORNUCOPIA
AMERICA AWAKE!
AMERICA'S DAFT ERA
ARTS OF PALEO FASTING
AUTOPHAGY ON CHEATERS
BACKSTABBING NEUROTICS
BETRAYAL TRAUMA
BOOMERS AND BROKENNESS
BOOT ON NECK
CHAMPION GUIDES
COMMIE NUTHOUSE
COMMIES
COMMUNIST SPIRIT
CONTAGION OF MADNESS
CONTAGIOUS MADNESS
CULTURE CLASH BASHED
DAFT LEFT
DAILY FASTARIAN
DAM RATS
DIVERSITY IS CRUELTY
E-RACE WHITE
EVIL FREAKS (Beyond Gross)
THE END OR A BEND?
FEMALE BULLIES AND FEMI-NAZIS
FEMALE CARNALITY
FEMALE DUMB DOWN
FEMALE POWER DRIVE
FEMINISM AND RUIN 1 & 2
FIX FOR MISFITS
FOOLS & TRAMPS
FREEDOM SPEAKING
FRENEMY ENABLER
FRENEMY LIAR
FRENEMY THIEF
FRENEMY TRAITOR
TRENEMY TYRANT
GENIUS IS HELD DOWN
GLOBALISLAM
GOD USES THE FLAWED
HAZE OF THE LATTER DAYS

THE HERD IN WORDS
HIX POLITIX
HOW THEY RUINED US
JUST SKIP DINNER
LE FEMME AND THE COMMUNIST SPIRIT
LIBERAL CHAOS & ROT
LIBERAL DOUBLETHINK
LIBERAL GALL 1 & 2
LIBERAL SHOVE-DOWNS
LOCK YOUR GATE
LOSERS and Femme Fatales
MANUAL FOR SUPERIOR MEN
MODERN ART FROM HELL
MOSTLY FAKE
NOTES TO CHAMPS 1 & 2
OVERCOME FRENEMIES
PC MAKES US CRAZY
PEOPLE ARE CRUEL
PEOPLE PROBLEMS 1 & 2
PERSECUTED GENIUIS
POLI-PSYCH MYSTERIES
PRETENTIOUS SLOBS
QUEEN BEE
RED NEW DEAL
RETURNING TO FIRST NATURE
SEASON OF TREASON
SEPARATE MEANS HOLY
SOCIAL HYPNOTISM
SOLITUDE SOLUTION
SUPERCILIOUS
THE SCHOOLS SCREWED EM UP
TOAD TO PRINCE
TRIALS CYCLES
TRUMP VS. GROUP
TRUST IN TRASH
THE TRUTH ABOUT PEOPLE
UNDERHEANDEDLY CLEVER
WALK TALL WITHIN WALLS
WE'RE NOT ALL ONE
WINNERS SKIP DINNER
WORK OR SMERK

AUTHOR BIO

Karen Kellock Ph.D.

Ph.D Political Psychology, UCI 1976
Post-Doctoral: UCI Medical School
Department of Psychiatry
Grants NIMH, NIAAA

Ph.D. dissertation "A Systems-Theoretic View of Pathologic Interaction" made an early mark as the "Wife of the Alcoholic Syndrome". Postdoctoral research at UCI Medical, Dept. of Psychiatry on the systems surrounding pathology on NIMH and NIAAA federal grants: *The Contagion of Madness: The Psychology of Neurotic Interaction and Pathological Systems*. Therapy tool Therapeutic Playwriting introduced the play *Mary and Murv: Gruesome Twosomes in the Alcoholic Marriage*. She taught Abnormal Psychology and Pathological Systems Theory at UC and CSU campuses and developed "the Debris Theory of Disease" in five books and website: (www.karenkellock.org): *Champion Guides, Daily Fastarian, Just Skip Dinner, Arts of Paleo Fasting, Ageless Cornucopia. Manual for Superior Men is a* pick-it-up-anywhere book that you can't put down (20,000 Kellockialisms) and ever on your desktop it should be found (or this Ebook for superior wordsearch of new jargon).